Rev. G. S. Corwin

Hebrew and American Slavery

Rev. G. S. Corwin

Hebrew and American Slavery

ISBN/EAN: 9783743321564

Manufactured in Europe, USA, Canada, Australia, Japa

Cover: Foto ©ninafisch / pixelio.de

Manufactured and distributed by brebook publishing software
(www.brebook.com)

Rev. G. S. Corwin

Hebrew and American Slavery

HEBREW

AND

AMERICAN SLAVERY.

———•———

A DISCOURSE,

By REV. G. S. CORWIN,

ELBA, N. Y.

———•———

ROCHESTER, N. Y.
PRESS OF A. STRONG & CO., DEMOCRAT AND AMERICAN OFFICE.
1863.

DISCOURSE.

Leviticus, xxv., 44–46.—"Both thy bondmen and thy bondsmaids, which thou shalt have, shall be of the heathen that are round about thee, of them shall ye buy bondmen and handmaids. Moreover, of the children of strangers that do sojourn among you, of them shall ye buy, and of their families that are with you which they begat in your land; and they shall be your possession,—and ye shall take them as an inheritance for your children after you to inherit them for a possession; and they shall be your bondmen forever."

SLAVERY is the great question of the day, of the nation, of the age; ought not every man to study it? It enters into almost every subject with which we have to do; ought we not to inform ourselves of its merits, its nature, and its workings? It has become, it is true, a political question—or has been—it is now more a national question, *i. e.* a question of national existence; but it is still a moral, a religious question, and proper for religious investigation. The fact that every man is required to act on it, makes it doubly important that every man should study it and be thoroughly acquainted with it. Politics are never so noble as when they grapple with some great moral subject, for then if men will be studious and honest, the national intellect will be enlarged and the national heart made better. But it will not do to say, a moral or a religious subject shall not be discussed in the pulpit when it becomes a political subject. The minister's duty is then the more imperious.

Two years and a half ago I found a paper lying on the desk, requesting me to comment on this text. I was at the time preaching a series of sermons on the sacred feasts and fasts of the Old Testament, and other institutions of the Mosaic law. I regarded it at the time a challenge to controvert, if I could, the doctrine of Slavery as here taught. I laid the paper aside, intending at a future time to preach from the text. It was then the summer before the election of President, and the question of Slavery entered very largely into the contest, and I judged that preaching on it at that time might and would be construed as a design on my part to meddle with politics. The position of things are changed. It has brought a civil war upon us, and it is not so much a question of politics as of national existence. It has brought the war upon us and has been hitherto the great sustaining power of the war against the Government. Every man is called on to judge whether it is right or wrong, whether our Government is acting right or wrong in resisting its demands, and in the blows it is dealing against it. Some say it is a Divine institution and we are fighting against God in defending ourselves against it. Secession preaches this doctrine, politicians preach it, the friends of Secession in the North preach it, ministers South and North preach it ; and if Slavery is right they have a right to, and they ought to. I find no fault with any one advocating it if he sincerely and *prayerfully* believe it right. But I do object to men professing to be honest in advocating, some for preaching it in the pulpit and denouncing others for saying a word against it. I protest against such a spirit as this —it is tyranny. I protest against such men's claims to consistency. I protest against any *such* claiming that it is *right*, for nothing that is *right* requires darkness, or hindering the honest expression of opinions. If it be right for Mr. Vandyke or Palmer to preach on the subject, where is the right of closing the mouths of other ministers, who by the Constitution and laws are guarantied equal rights ? Men who do this virtually admit the unsoundness of the doctrines they hold ; and expose the tyranny they would exercise over the consciences of men. And these are the men who as a general thing are the most noisy against our Government for doing it in extreme cases.

The text is a part of a system of laws designed for a particular people, for a particular age and circumstances, and was not designed for our age of the world nor for any nation of the present day. They ceased to be binding even on the Jews after the death of Christ. In this system of law are enjoined three annual feasts, binding on the whole nation ; eating a lamb with bitter herbs and unleavened bread for seven days, circumcision of every male child on the eighth day after its birth ; the sacrificing of lambs, bullocks, goats, birds ; cities of refuge for the manslayer to flee to, &c. &c.

The Jews for whom the law was made were not allowed to take any interest for money loaned to a Jew, if he was embarrassed ; they were required to marry a deceased brother's widow ; they were permitted to divorce their wives for mere caprice or dislike, and marry others ; there was no prohibition in this law against polygamy, and this for a time was generally practiced even by their best men ; they were forbidden to eat swine's flesh, and certain other animals, and birds. None of these laws are now incorporated into the codes of civilized or Christianized nations. None of them are binding on Jew or Gentile. Most of them are prohibited by law with Christian nations. Men would now be imprisoned for doing what Abraham, Jacob, David, Solomon, and the Jews generally did.

Why then should we appeal to this law to justify Slavery when we would not allow the Mormon or the Free-lover to appeal to it to justify divorce or polygamy? The advocates of Slavery appeal to the Patriarchs in justification of it ; the Mormons appeal to the Patriarchs in justification of polygamy. Does the conduct of the Patriarchs justify the one more than the other? Abraham held slaves, therefore Slavery is right. Abraham had a child by one of his slaves, therefore adultery is right. The one is no more condemned than the other and no more justified than the other, in anything said about Abraham. Jacob had two wives and two concubines, and not a word is said against it, therefore polygamy is a Divine institution. The Jew was allowed to divorce his wife for personal dislike, and this he might repeat as often as he pleased for there is no restriction ; and this is all the Free-lover asks. And by the arguments used for Slavery we must justify Mormonism, Free-loveism, polygamy, concubinage, and adultery. All the Mulattoes, Quadroons, Octoroons of the South, two millions or more, have as honorable parentage as Ishmael, so far as marriage is concerned, and are a part of the Divine institution. If a Patriarch's practice may be appealed to to justify one wrong it may be to justify another. The Mormon and the Free-lover have just as good arguments for their systems as the Slave-holder has for his, in the conduct of the Patriarchs.

" Happy is he that condemneth not himself in that thing which he alloweth." Are any of the advocates of Slavery willing their sons-in-law should put away their daughters and marry other women ? or take other wives or concubines to share the conjugal honors and emoluments with their daughters? If not, they are advocates of a system for others which they will not allow for themselves. Yes, they approve for others what they would regard a great wrong—an outrage on themselves. Are these men willing their sons should be sold into Slavery? But this was a part of the law. The text commands or permits rather, purchasing and holding as slaves the heathen about them, but the system permitted them to enslave one another, not only for six years, but for life or till the year of Jubilee. "If thou buy a Hebrew servant, six years shall he serve, and in the seventh year he shall go out for nothing. If he came in by himself he shall go out by himself; if he were married then his wife shall go out with him. If his master have given him a wife, and she have borne him sons or daughters, the wife and her children shall be her masters and he shall go out by himself. And if the servant shall plainly say, I love my master, my wife and my children, I will not go out free ; then his master shall bring him unto the judges, and he shall also bring him unto the door or unto the door-post, and his master shall bore his ear through with an awl, and he shall serve him forever."—Ex., xxi. 2-6. The Hebrews might enslave each other for debt, that is, compel to service, (See Lev., xxv. 39.); to be held till the year of release or jubilee ; and the wife and children might be held as servants to one of these periods, according to the law ; and if the man was not willing to leave his wife and children he might become a servant himself till their time expired. Thus the poor were subjected to this kind of slavery and subjected their children to it. Are any of the advocates of Slavery willing to abide by this law? which is very much better than our laws on Slavery. Most families have some poor among them. What father or mother is willing that their poor son should be a slave for his poverty? Every man who would do to others as he would that others should do to him, ought never to appeal to the Mosaic law for what he would regard as a great injustice if put in force with him or his children. Such an appeal furnishes a very strong argument against his honesty, his humanity, and especially against his Christianity—for this is the law of Christianity—the digest, the sum and substance of all her laws as well as the test of the Christian ; to love our neighbor as ourselves, and if there is any doubt about any duty, the justice of any law or practice, we are to try it by this rule:—Would it be a good law if practiced on us? Are we willing to abide by it? If not we expose ourselves when we advocate it for others.

Our argument is not against the Mosaic law as a bad law, but against justifying any *wrong* by *that law ;* a law made for another people and under entirely different circumstances. Two things especially are wrong with us on this point :

1st. For a people with our opportunities, our intelligence, the light of the age in which we live, to appeal to the laws of a people just emerging from heathenism and bondage, living in the darkest age of the world and in the midst of all forms of wickedness consequent thereon.

2d. Appealing to laws to justify what is a great deal worse than anything found in those laws. Our system of Slavery is not the Scripture system but the heathen in its worst form. Whoever will be at the trouble to compare will not fail to see how little it resembles the one and how much it resembles the other. It differs from the Mosaic system in these particulars :

I. Hebrew Slavery permitted the enslaving of any for

debt; the man might sell himself, Lev. xxv. 39 ; a father might sell his children, Ex. xxi. 7 ; insolvent debtors might be delivered to their creditors as slaves, 2. Kings, iv. 1 ; thieves not able to make restitution were sold for the benefit of the injured party, Ex. xxii., 3 ; prisoners taken in war of the heathen nations about them, Lev. xxv. 44, 46. In all these cases, if we except the last, which we will presently consider, there is some propriety—at least a show of justice. The man who has had value received and in debt for it, ought to pay it if he can; and if he has not the money ought to labor for it, if he is able; and if he will not, deserves to be made to do it. The Hebrew law of debt would not be a bad one for us. It would empty many a bar-room ; prevent much extravagance and dishonesty in contracting debts ; greatly diminish the tenants of our poor-houses, jails and prisons ; prevent a vast deal of idleness, vice and crime ; make great numbers honest men who are now rogues ; save a vast amount of money to the Government ; and give a security against public and private thieves, which is very much needed, and a sense of security in person and property which would add very much to the comfort and happiness of society. Slavery for thieving, we have no objections to, and I doubt whether any but rogues have. Would it not be better to make a man work and pay twice or three times the amount stolen than to lock him up in jail and maintain him there at the public expense, taxing the innocent to pay for the crimes of the guilty? No one is benefited by this process—neither the loser of the stolen property, the person imprisoned nor his family, and the public is the loser in all the expenses incurred. Our State prison laws (in the Free States) are founded on the Jewish law. We make men slaves for a number of years in proportion to their crimes, the amount they have stolen or the mischief they have done. This part of the Jewish law was right—absolutely better than our jail system.

But our Slave code has no resemblance to this. It is not founded on justice, nor in the slightest show or pretence to justice. It is not for debt, and it is not for crime. The

Southern slave owed his master nothing and had never wronged him, never stole a farthing from him but was himself stolen ; and the difference between the two systems on this point is the difference between *enslaving* a man for *stealing*, and *stealing* a man to *enslave* him ; between making a man pay his honest debts, and making him labor to support idleness and crime in others ; between enslaving him for his own wrong doing and enslaving an innocent man for the villany of others ; it is the difference between the honest man who pays his laborer for services rendered and the infamous villain who forces another to labor for nothing.

II. Stealing men for slaves was forbidden and punished with death by the Hebrew code. Our Slavery is of this character exclusively. " And he that stealeth a man and selleth him, or if he be found in his hand, he shall surely be put to death," Ex. xxi., 16. The Jews might purchase a man —if he was willing to sell himself, or if he was sold for debt or crime, he might purchase those held in Slavery by the heathen, and enslave the heathen taken captive in war. These were the only sources of Slavery to the Jew. Our Slavery comes from none of these sources. Our slaves are stolen men and women—stolen by those who hold them, or purchased from those who stole them or who were hired to steal them. They have been kidnapped in Africa and in our own country. American Slavery began with the Roman Catholic Spaniard in the darkest age of that darkest system of human iniquity. It was devised as a substitute for slavery of the Indians who were found unable to endure the hardships of Spanish Slavery, and by that system of religion which made merchandise of "the bodies and souls of men," or as it is translated, " slaves and souls of men," Rev. xviii., 13, and which by God is doomed to perdition. The origin of the system is this : "In order to provide some remedy for this, (enslaving the Indians,) without which he found it was in vain to maintain his scheme, Las Casas proposed to purchase a sufficient number of negroes from the Portuguese settlement, on the coast of Africa, and to transport them to

America in order that they might be employed as slaves in working the mines and tilling the ground. Various circumstances concurred in reviving this odious commerce (in slaves), which had been long abolished in Europe, and which is no less repugnant to the feelings of humanity than to the principles of religion. As early as the year 1503, a few negro slaves had been sent into the New World. In the year 1511, Ferdinand permitted the importation of them in greater numbers;" and Charles in greater numbers still, and so it went on to increase to its present magnitude.— Robertson's Am., I., 209. There is not a word of license in the Scriptures for this. It was wholly a question of interest with those who engaged in it. The negro could endure more than the Indian, and this was their warrant, and it is ours—and all the one we have. The law of Moses would consign all engaged in this business to the gallows. The whole system was a system of kidnapping—man stealing; and every means was taken to steal men, women and children. Their dwellings were set on fire by night, villages set on fire and the fleeing, helpless inhabitants caught and sold for slaves! Wars were made to catch slaves, the land desolated for this object alone—and men—strange as fiction, Bible men, Christian ministers call this a Divine institution! Will they show where Moses or God authorized making war on an unoffending people to make slaves of them? or firing a dwelling by night to catch the inmates for slaves? or knocking men down and gagging them and selling them for slaves, as has been done in hundreds if not thousands of instances in our own land? This is our system. It had its origin in cupidity, in the lowest, worst passions of man's fallen nature, and like Mormonism and most other falsehoods craves justification from the Bible.

III. Hebrew Slavery was not a system of traffic in human beings ; ours is ; the Hebrew slave when bought had a home secured to him till the year of release or the year of jubilee. Ours has no security that he shall not to-morrow be sold into another part of the country and be separated from his wife and children.

In our text the Jews were permitted to buy slaves, but the text cannot be found where they are permitted to sell them; neither can a *case* be found except Joseph, which is recorded as a crime of the darkest hue. When the slave was bought he became a part of the family and a permanent fixture in the family till the year of release or the year of jubilee. He must be educated as one of the family, be circumcised corrected, religiously instructed the same as the children of the family, and he must remain in the family as one of its members till he is made free. There is no law in the Hebrew code for selling slaves, no permission as there is for buying, no provision, no intimation of a right to sell or a recorded case of sale.

Our system is one of traffic, speculation, buying and sell, ing to make money. Like the Harlot of Rome, we trade in "beasts, and sheep, and horses, and chariots, *and slaves, and the souls of men.*" The laws of all the Slave States authorize the sale of slaves, for debt, or at the will of the master. The slaves, male or female, are put up at auction on the slave block, often naked or nearly so, that the purchaser may see if there is any defect. They are purchased by slave-traders, kept in slave-pens or prisons till a day of sale, or till they can be transferred to another market.

In Virginia, for several years, slaves have been raised for the Southern market; and this has been one of her sources of wealth. One of the reasons assigned by some of her public men why she should go with the Southern Confederacy was that her interest was with the South; it was her market for her Slaves.

And our system on this point shows no regard to the laws of God or humanity. The husband is separated from his wife and family, mothers from their children, brothers and sisters from each other, and sold into distant parts with no more regard to the laws of God on marriage, or the laws of humanity, than if we were a nation of Turks or Mormons. On the score of humanity we ought to be ashamed to look a Mormon in the face. He has not added this disgrace to his system, of selling his own children.

IV. The Jewish code of Slavery was mild and humane; ours is the most inhuman and tyrannical system at this day on the face of the earth, and holds rank with any that has ever existed, in its oppression and severity. An injury to the Hebrew slave secured him his liberty. "And if a man smite the eye of his servant or the eye of his maid that it perish, he shall *let him go free* for his eye's sake. And if he smite out his man servant's tooth or his maid servant's tooth, he shall let him go for his tooth's sake."—Ex. xxi., 26, 27. By this law he was protected from injury. Again, if his master oppressed him or made his servitude harsh or such as he was unwilling to endure, he might run away, and the law forbade any to deliver him up. "Thou shalt not deliver unto his master the servant which is escaped from his master unto thee ; thou shalt not oppress him."— Deut. xxiii., 15, 16. You shall not send him back to be oppressed nor oppress him yourself. The passage in Ex. xxi., 20, 21, is the only one which looks like American Slavery in all the Bible : "If a man smite his servant or his maid with a rod and he die under his hand, he shall be surely punished. Notwithstanding if he continue a day or two he shall not be punished, for he is his money." The punishment of murder was death, and there was no exceptions made as to who was murdered. See Lev. xxiv., 21, 22. If the man killed his slave he was to be put to death ; if he lived he lost his property; for it is enacted in verses 26 and 27, of this same chapter (Ex. xxi.) and of the same persons, that if they only suffered the loss of an eye or a tooth they had their liberty ; the man was fined and not executed, for his cruelty. If our Slave laws were as good as this and had been put in practice, probably more than a million of our slaves would be free ; this number, at least, we doubt not have been maltreated. If there were any evidences of intention to murder, the man was to be put to death ; if in the anger of the moment he killed him, he was to be punished for manslaughter; if the slave lived he lost him; his cruelty secured him his liberty. The law did not differ materially from some of our Free State laws and with persons who are not slaves. Men are here, in the State of New York, executed for murder (when we can find judges and jurors honest enough to execute the law), imprisoned for manslaughter and fined for injury done their neighbors. Some suppose it had reference only to those slaves who were heathen, and that God allowed this severity only to this class. They are one and the same, as will be seen by reading the passage. The whipping and the loss of the eye and the tooth are spoken of servants—and the same servants whether they be Jew or heathen, or both ; let those who wish to make something more or less than the truth out of it determine. Again, God forbid all harsh treatment to the stranger, to all who embraced the Jewish religion, without regard to their position or circumstances. "Judge righteously between every man and his brother and the *stranger* that is with you."—Deut. i., 16. " God regardeth not persons ; He doth execute the judgment of the fatherless and widow, and loveth the *stranger ; love ye therefore the stranger ;* for ye were strangers in the land of Egypt."—Deut. x., 17, 19. " The *stranger* that dwelleth with you shall be unto you as one born among you, and thou shalt love him as thyself."—Lev. ix., 34. " *Thou* shalt neither *vex a stranger* nor *oppress him.*"—Ex. xxii., 21. " Thou shalt not *oppress a stranger,* for ye know the heart of a stranger."—Ex. xxiii., 9. " Cursed be he that *perverteth* the *judgment* of a *stranger.*"—Deut. xxvii., 19.

Nothing like these provisions is found in our system of Slavery. There is no law against the most wanton cruelty which is not a dead law on the statute book. It is not known that a master has ever been executed for killing his slave, or that a slave has any claim by law, to his liberty for maltreatment, however severe, even to maiming. The slave, in our system, has no remedy—no appeal for injuries done him by his master. He cannot even testify as to what he or his fellow-slaves suffer by their masters. They have been whipped to death, starved to death, died from want of clothing and ill usage, and they have no remedy—none to help. I state these facts on the testimony of the Rev. Geo. Whitfield,

Rev. Jonathan Edwards, their members of Congress, their own newspapers, cases in their Courts of law, Southern men, and men of unimpeachable character who have witnessed these things. If one escapes from bondage, however he may have been whipped, or torn and maimed by dogs or by shooting him, he must be restored to his master to be whipped and tortured to his heart's desire ; and God appealed to as the author of the system! It is made a penal offence to harbor a slave, as in the old heathen laws of Rome, while Mosaic law made it a duty.

V. Hebrew Slavery was by express permission and direction of God for a people under very different circumstances and surroundings from ours, and our Slavery is without any such permission. Slavery was universally practised in that dark and barbarous age of the world. The Jews themselves had just emerged from a state of bondage, ignorant, sensual, vicious, as all who are brutalized by Slavery are to a greater or less degree. Their ancestors were taken from among the heathen a few centuries before, taught something of the true God, which was transmitted by tradition and hieroglyphics, for we have no evidence that they had any written language at the time, and they themselves had been in bondage to an idolatrous nation, more ignorant than themselves, for more than two hundred years. It would be strange if they, with such surroundings and circumstances, should not have been idolatros, sensualists, a " stiff necked and rebellious people," ignorant, vicious and cruel. This is just what they were. They lived in an age of great darkness and ignorance, and they were ignorant and blinded by the darkness which surrounded them. They saw nothing but Slavery, and no wonder they should think it right. They had lived for no higher object than the gratification of sense, as this is all any slave without religion has to live for ; no wonder they should be sensualists and prefer " the flesh-pots," " the fish which they did eat in Egypt freely ; the cucumbers, and the melons, and the leeks, and the onions, and the garlick." With no written language, no bible, no books, and but few instructors, and these with but little knowledge of

God ; everywhere seeing Slavery, idolatry, polygamy, concubinage, divorce, with no law against them, no wonder they should be in favor with all these, and with their fallen natures uncurbed by religion, should resist the sudden overthrow of all this by law. This was the condition of the people to whom the Mosaic law of Slavery, of divorce, of polygamy, was given. It was good, the best that could be done for them. It was just or nearly what has had to be done, or what has been done with the savages to whom the gospel has been sent. Will the Slave-owners or the advocates of Slavery admit this to be their condition? Is such a law necessary for them? or has God given them the codes which they practice? We know that the system of American Slavery is incomparably worse than the old Jewish system, and to be justified by that, the people ought to be incomparably worse—be more ignorant, brutalized, debased and vicious. Is their system given them by God? then it is the best God could give them, for God does that which is best under the circumstances. What then must be the state of that people with such a system of Slavery as exists in the South? Does God authorize those laws which forbid teaching the slave to read the Bible? which imprisons ministers for preaching it? and even females for teaching its precepts? None but barbarians have ever had such a system of laws, and if Southerners are not, they are an exception. God allowed no such laws as are found on the statute books of our Slave code, to the Jews with all their darkness, idolatry and sensuality. Which of these dilemmas will Slavery take? If God authorized their system and gave them the best that their moral and intellectual condition would admit of, they must be a very benighted, sensual, cruel, beastly people ; but if God did not authorize the system they must be a great deal worse ; be all this and knaves to boot, for they claim God for their system. The laws themselves prove the authors of them to be a very cruel, unjust, Godless, graceless, heartless, barbarous people. No such laws are found on the statute books of any but such a people. Heathenism in its worst forms had but few things worse on this subject. That

I have not misconstrued the Jewish law, we adduce the Saviour's exposition of it. The Jews—the Pharisees, for these are the men who are for tight laws for others and loose ones for themselves—appealed to Moses for the law of divorce, —the right to put away a wife for any personal dislike. The Saviour answered them : " Moses, *because of the hardness of your hearts, suffered you* to put away your wives, but from the beginning it was not so. And I say unto you, whosoever shall put away his wife, except for fornication, and shall marry another, committeth adultery."—Math. xix., 3, 9. This was a part of the Mosaic law, and like the rest of it adapted to the circumstances of the Jews at the time it was made. The thing was allowed as a part of their civil polity, not because it was right in itself, but because circumstances made it necessary. " Moses found the custom in use. He found a hard-hearted and rebellious people. In this state of things he did not deem it prudent to forbid a practice so universal," but did the best he could for the people under the circumstances. Among some heathen nations to whom the gospel has been carried, who had never known anything but polygamy and slavery, something has been allowed to those who had several wives and held slaves when converted to Christianity ; and if our Slave-holders are in this condition something may be allowed to them. The Saviour's exposition of the law is not very creditable to the intelligence and virtue of any who practice or appeal to the law to justify their conduct and sentiments. " Because of the *hardness of your hearts*, Moses *suffered* you ;" because of *wickedness*, your *love of wrong*, your *insensibility* to *what was right ;* because of your *perverse will* to do what *was wrong*, and *hatred* and *resistance* of *what was right ;* because of your *enmity* to God's holy law, written on the tables of stone, and delivered by God himself on Mount Sinai ; Moses allowed you to depart from that law, the spirit of it at least ; but I say unto you, the man who practices Moses' law of divorce is guilty of adultery, and by the same rule the man who enslaves another is guilty of robbery and the worst kind of robbery—for he robs a man of his inalienable rights,—" Life, liberty, and the pursuit of happiness ;" robs him of the most precious of God's gifts to him,—his wife and children,—of his own manhood! and, no wonder, when he has gone thus far that he can appeal to God to justify the sin.

The questions for those to settle who plead the Mosaic law as a justification for modern Slavery, are :

1st. Is the law still in force, or is it permitted to those to whom it was originally given? If it is, the Jews have a right to enslave the heathen now,—any heathen,—white or black, all that do not embrace the Jewish religion, and ourselves among the rest. We are not Jews. Nor do we embrace their religion as these Pharisees held it. If it be said it was given to the Church, and we have been engrafted into the Jewish Church, and are therefore entitled to its privileges, from which the Jews were cut off, then we may enslave the Irish, the German, the Indian, any who do not embrace the religion ; any who are too poor to pay their debts, or guilty of theft or other crimes, and hold them for fifty years ; then all who are members of the Church, and are slaves, are entitled to their liberty at the end of six years ; for if we adopt the system or claim it as ours, we must have a year of release every seventh year, and a jubilee every fiftieth year. In this case, the laws of all the Free States, on the subject of Slavery are wrong. May we select such parts of the system as suit us? The Mormon and Free-lover have selected theirs, and the Slave-holder has selected his, but is by no means as near the original law and practice as the Mormon.

2d. Did God, authorizing the Jews four thousand years since to do certain things, authorize us to do the same or similar things? He authorized the Jews utterly to exterminate the Canaanites and Amalekites. Does this authorize us to exterminate the Indians, the Mexicans, or any nation? If not, upon what grounds do we plead the practices, permissions or laws given to another people under entirely different circumstances?

The Saviour has answered both these questions in his

2.

reply to the Pharisees, who would perpetuate a system suited
to their prejudices and their wickedness ; and his answer
carries with it an exposition of the law, and a tremendous
rebuke to all who take shelter under it for Slavery, polygamy
and slippery divorces. His answer shows that the law was
made, and was fit only for men who would not endure a
better one—men shrouded in moral darkness and surrounded with the wrongs which were tolerated; and he pronounced
it 'inoperative, null and void to the Jews themselves; in the
better state of things to which they had arrived.

VI. The Mosaic code of Slavery was designed to ameliorate the condition of the slave, elevate him to manhood, make
him intelligent, and fit him for usefulness ; our system in all
its laws and workings is calculated and designed to brutalize the slave, to work manhood out of him, to keep him
ignorant, and to debase him and convert him from a man
to a thing.

1st. In the Hebrew system he was to be educated in their
religion and admitted to all its privileges and advantages.
" And he that is eight days old shall be circumcised among
you, every man child in your generations, he that is born in
thy house or *bought with money of any stranger which is
not of thy seed.* He that is born in thy house and he that
is bought with thy money must needs be circumcised ; and
my covenant shall be *in your flesh* for an everlasting covenant." This was the seal of membership to the covenant
made with Abraham, and secured them the privileges of
that covenant. These slaves or servants were *instructed* in
the *Jewish religion*, went with their masters to *the Passover*,
and all the great *religious festivals* of the Jews, heard the
reading of the law, and had all the precepts of the law not
only *taught* them, but they were *compelled* to keep them the
same as their children. Ex. xxiii., 14-17, and xxxiv., 23. " The
slaves were likewise guests in the family festivals." " And
there shall ye eat before the Lord your God, and ye shall
rejoice in all that ye put your hands unto, *ye and your
households*, wherein the Lord thy God hath blessed thee,

and ye shall rejoice before the Lord your God, ye and your sons, and your daughters, and *your menservants*, and *your maidservants*, and the Levite that is within thy gates."—Deut. xii., 7, 12. The whole family was included in these religious festivals. The slaves shared equally with the children in the religious instruction, in the festivity, in all the advantages of their whole religious system. In one of these great national convocations, Moses thus addressed them : " Ye stand this day all of you before the Lord your God ; your captains of your tribes, your elders and your officers, with all the men of Israel, your little ones, your wives, and *the stranger* that is in thy camp, *from the hewer of thy wood unto the drawer of thy water;* that thou shouldst enter into covenant with the Lord thy God, and unto his oath which the Lord thy God maketh with thee this day." Deut. xxix. 10—12. All congregated together, the master and his servant, all received the same instruction, all entered together into covenant with God, all ate together, all rejoiced together, all had a mutual interest, and shared in each other's welfare.

Nothing like this is found in our system, but the very reverse of it all. The laws of South Carolina forbid *any assemblage* of *slaves* for the purpose of *mental instruction*, and the magistrates are required to disperse any assemblage of slaves, free negroes, mulattoes and mestizores, and authorizes inflicting corporeal punishment not exceeding twenty lashes. They are not permitted to meet even with white persons for the purpose of *mental instruction*. (Brevard Dig. 254-5.) The laws of Virginia are the same, imposing twenty lashes to any such persons. In Georgia they impose ten days' imprisonment and thirty-nine lashes. In North Carolina, to teach a slave to read or write, or sell, or give him any book, (the Bible not excepted,) or pamphlet, is punished with thirty-nine lashes or imprisonment. (Law of 1831.) In Georgia, if a white teach a slave to write, he is fined five hundred dollars, and imprisoned at the discretion of the Court. A father may be flogged for teaching his own child. (Law of 1829.) Kentucky and Maryland are the only

States in which education is not forbidden to the slaves. The spirit and design of it are shown in a speech of Mr. Berry, in the Virginia House of Delegates in 1832. "We have," said Mr. Berry, "*as far as possible, closed every avenue by which light might enter the minds of slaves. If we could extinguish the capacity to see the light, our work would be completed; they would then be on a level with the beasts of the field, and we should be safe! I am not certain that we would not do it if we could find out the process, and that on the plea of necessity.*"

Ministers have been imprisoned, females have been imprisoned, and treated with all kinds of hardships and abuse for teaching slaves to read the Bible. These cases have become quite numerous of late years, and barbarous enough we should think to satisfy even a slave driver's appetite for cruelty.

2d. The Jewish law made the slave a man, regarded him a man, treated him as man; our laws make him a chattel, a mere beast of burthen, not a man but a thing. By the Jews he was treated with respect, worshipped with the family, eat with the family, sat with the family, was entrusted with the interests of the family, sometimes married into the family, and the children of them became the heirs of the master. Abram did not treat Hager's son as Southern masters do their children by their slaves, sell them into bondage. Jacob's children, by Bilhah and Zilpah, his wives slaves, were made equal with his children by Leah and Rachael. Eliezer, Abram's servant, was entrusted with the oversight of all his property, sent with wealth and authority to select a wife for his son, was received into the family of Bethuel, and treated as the plenipotentiary of a great prince. "Samuel took Saul and *his servant,* and brought them into the *parlor,* and made *them* sit in the *chiefest* place, among them that were bidden, which were about thirty persons," 1. Sam. ix. 22. One of our slaves would have found a place in the kitchen. Ziba, Saul's servant, had twenty servants of his own, and large estates, 2. Sam. ix. 10. In 1. Chron. ii. 34—35, we find this history of a slave: "Now Sheshan had no sons but daughters. And Sheshan had a *servant*, an *Egyptian*, whose name was Jarha, and Sheshan gave his daughter to Jarha, his *servant* to wife, and she bare him Attai." What shameless amalgamationists those Hebrews were! They not only married with their slaves, but elevated them to posts of honor. The grandson of this Attai was made a noble in David's army. 1. Chron. xi. 11.

Our slave laws do not recognize slaves as men, but as chattels. The decisions of our Slave Judges are, that they have no rights as men, no religious, no civil rights. Judge Crenshaw decided that: " A slave is in absolute bondage. *He has no civil rights.*" Stewart's Ala. Rep. 320. "*Slaves are deprived of all civil rights.*" Judge Mathews, in Martin's Lou. Rep. 559. Chief Justice Taney has decided that " the slave has no rights which white men are bound to respect." He is not a citizen, and has no rights as a man. And the whole system of American Slavery is calculated and designed to degrade him from a man to a brute. If he is permitted to go into church, he must go into the negro's pew in some out of the way corner. If he comes to the Lord's table, he must sit by himself. In the family, he never eats with the family—never permitted to sit with the family —nor be educated with the family, and even in the Free States is excluded from the schools of the whites. The whole system of American Slavery is a studied effort to degrade the slave, to work manhood and humanity out of him, to make him feel that he is an inferior being, and servitude the place for which God created him. We degrade him, debase him, brutalize him, and then excuse ourselves for enslaving him by the argument that he is an inferior race! What would they be who boastingly use this argument, if they were in the slaves' place a few hundred years? The argument itself shows that they are below many of them now in reasoning powers. He must be more than a man, who would not be inferior by such usage as the slave receives, and surrounded with such circumstances as he is and has always been.

VII. The Jews made provision for giving freedom to their slaves ; all our provisions are to make Slavery perpetual ; the Jewish system abridged it, ameliorated and abolished it ; ours intensifies it in severity, perpetuates and extends it. If a Jew was sold for debt, or for crime, he received his freedom in the year of release, or at the end of six years at the longest. Exod. xxi. 2. If he sold himself through extreme poverty, he could be held only till the year of Jubilee. Lev. xxv. 39—41. In this year was proclaimed throughout the land, universal freedom. This year—every fiftieth year, all were made free, and all lands reverted to their ancient owners. "And ye shall hallow the fiftieth year, and proclaim *liberty throughout all the land, unto all the inhabitants thereof.* It shall be a jubilee unto you, and ye shall return every man unto his possession, and unto his family." Lev. xxv. 8—11.

From the passage in Lev. xxv. 46, " They shall be your bondmen forever," it is argued, that slaves purchased from the heathen did not receive their liberty in the year of Jubilee. That this is not correct, is evident from these considerations :

1st. That the word *forever*, is frequently used in a limited sense, and is here. Lev. x. 15, "And it shall be thine, and thy sons with thee by a statute *forever.*" But this statute has long since ceased. 1. Saml. i. 22, "Then will I bring him, that he may appear before the Lord, and there abide forever," in the temple at Shiloh, with Eli. But he abode there only during his life ; and *forever*, here meant only as long as he lived. Josh. iv. 7, "And these stones shall be for a memorial unto the children of Israel forever ;" for a long time. In Exod. xxi. 6, it means till the year of Jubilee, as is plain by comparing it with Lev. xxv. 39—41. In Exod. xxi. 6, it is ordained that the Jew was made a slave *forever* by a certain act of his ; and in Lev. xxv. 41—54, it is shown that this *forever* means only till the year of Jubilee.

2d. The word *forever* is just as long with the heathen slave as with the Jewish, and *no longer.* If it meant to the

Jubilee in the one case, it did in the other; for it is applied to both classes of slaves. In Exod. xxv. 6, it is ordained of the *Jew*, that " he shall serve him, (his master,) *forever.*" In Lev. xxv. 46, it is ordained of *heathen slaves*, " they shall be your bondmen *forever.*" Is *forever* in the one case any longer than the other? If it be limited in the one, and not the other, it must be by some enactment or explanation which cannot be found.

3d. Freedom in the Jubilee is proclaimed to all. "And ye shall *proclaim liberty* throughout all the land"—to whom? to all the Jewish slaves? to all of a particular class who are enslaved? No, but " to *all the inhabitants thereof*," to all in bondage, to all whom it concerned; " the stranger that is in thy camp, the hewer of thy wood, and drawer of thy water."

4th. It is proved by its results—it broke up Slavery, as doubtless it was designed to do, and as such laws inevitably would. We find no evidence that Slavery existed among the Jews after Nehemiah's day—and then it was only Jewish oppression; Jews oppressing Jews, and not foreigners. They evidently had no foreign slaves at this time, and there is no mention in any of their writers or writings of Slavery, until the gospel came in contact with the heathen nations, in and after Christ's day; and this accounts for Christ saying nothing about it. While it existed, the prophets severely rebuked it, denounced its wickedness, the displeasure of God against it, and as one of the causes of their being sold into Slavery. Ish. i. 17; lviii. 6—7. Ezek. xxii. 29; xxxiv. 17.

We have considered Jewish Slavery from the brief laws and notices of it as recorded in the Bible in the beginning of that nation, emerging from a state of Slavery themselves, and entirely surrounded with it in an age of great moral darkness; but to justify our Slavery by theirs, it should be when they had made their greatest attainments in religion and Christian knowledge. Though they never had the light and advantages we have, they had enough to abolish Slavery. Their laws, made more than three thousand years ago, in all their semi-barbarism, had religion, virtue and humanity enough in them to undermine and destroy this more than barbarous practice of enslaving their fellow men. The careful study of the Bible on this institution, cannot fail to convince us how grossly it is misunderstood—and sweep away the infidel's cavil against its inspiration. If our Slavery is Bible Slavery, the infidel has a valid argument for his infidelity, for if God is the author of such a system, he is a monster whom all would fear, but none could love. None who will look at the difference will fail to see how little they resemble each other, and how absurd, disingenuous at least, to justify the one by the other. Hebrew Slavery existed in an age of great darkness, three thousand years ago ; ours in the full sunshine of gospel knowledge. Theirs was the best that could be done under the circumstances ; ours is the worst that can be under the circumstances. Theirs was for debts contracted by the man himself, for crimes committed; ours is for neither debt nor crime. Theirs was for a righteous claim or a just punishment ; ours is without the pretense of either. When purchased of the heathen, or taken prisoners in war, they were educated in the Jewish religion, made members in the family ; our slaves are stolen, kidnapped, and denied a religious education, or a family membership. Man-stealing in the Jewish system, was punished with death ; ours is a system of man-stealing entirely. Theirs was not a system of traffic in human beings ; ours is. Theirs was mild and humane ; ours is cruel and oppressive in the extreme. Theirs was by express permission of God, or direction of God ; we have no such permission or direction. Theirs was designed to ameliorate the state of Slavery then prevalent in the world ; ours is no improvement on Slavery anywhere existing, but is worse than any system found in the civilized world. Theirs was designed and calculated to elevate the slave to manhood ; ours is designed and calculated to work manhood out of the slave, and brutalize him. They made him a man ; we make him a chattel. The Jewish system made provision for the slave's freedom; ours makes every possible provision against it. Theirs grew milder, and disappeared from among them as they gained light; ours has increased and extended in the midst of light, and has grown worse instead of better. Theirs was a mild, Christian system; ours is a cruel, heathen system. Theirs worked its own cure by a wise legislation; ours is working its cure by its monstrous wickedness, and is washing itself out in blood. Theirs ceased by doing right about it, giving the slave his freedom, as England and other Christian States have done; ours is ending as it did in Egypt, and other heathen nations in the Red Sea.

I have used the words *slave* and *slavery* in running a parallel between American Slavery and the old Jewish code of service, because the advocates of slavery claim the Jewish code as a system of slavery, and justify American Slavery by it ; but in truth, the Jewish system was not slavery in any sense as we now use the term. The term *servant*, as used in the Old Testament writers, is not *slave*, in the sense we use the word. It did not convey to the Jew the idea of *chattel, thing, brute animal*, but a man or a woman bound to service for a time. The framers of our National Constitution would not allow the terms *slave* and *slavery* in that instrument, and thereby refused to recognize what the term slave is now meant to imply—ownership of men, and the destruction of the rights of man, the converting of a man to a thing—a beast of burthen—a thing without rights, absolutely, unconditionally the property of another, a creature to be regarded in no other light than the amount of money he will bring in the market, or the amount of labor he can perform. This is the meaning of slave as now defined by Southern law, and maintained by their courts of law. In this sense the Jews never held slaves—they never had any such laws as these, and to charge it upon them is the grossest slander.

The teachings, the laws, the institutions of the Old Testament are all against Slavery—opposed to all oppression. This is the declaration of their learned men, Maimonides, and others. It is found in their prophets and sacred writings, coupled with threatenings and denunciations. Prov. xxii.

22—23. Ish. i. 17; v. 7—9 ; xxx. 12—13 ; lxviii. 6. Jer. xxxiv. 17. Ezek. xxii. 29—31, and chapter xxxiv. Learned and able writers on Jewish law assure us, that there is in Hebrew no *word for slave* in the sense we use it, and the laws of Moses no where recognizes such a right in man as slaveholders claim. Able and learned Jewish writers show conclusively that the Mosaic law was much milder than it appears to us, designed for the general good of the poor and the oppressed, and worked out the problem it designed, of elevating and freeing them.

A careful examination of the Mosaic laws will convince us:

1st. That there was no slavery in the modern sense of the word among the Jews ; and

2d. Therefore no slave insurrections, as in every nation where Slavery has prevailed; in Sicily, Rome, Crete, Sparta, Thessaly, Hayti, and the United States.

3d. That their laws of service prevented pauperism, vagrancy, idleness, &c. We find no mention of poor-houses, alms-houses, jails, prisons, beggars, and the like. Their remedy for poverty was work, for insolvency work and pay the debt, for theft, work. They carried out God's law, "six days shalt thou labor," and made all comply with it ; and this was much better, and accomplished more in preventing poverty, bankruptcy and crime, than all modern improvements for these evils.

Since our attention has been called to the subject, we must not dismiss it without noticing the teachings of the New Testament. It is claimed that Christ said nothing against it, and therefore he approved it. It is certain Christ said nothing *for it*, and never manifested any interest for it, then how comes it, that those who profess to follow his example can say so much for it, and manifest so deep an interest in it? If Christ said nothing against it, it was because it was not necessary he should, for it did not exist, was not practiced by those to whom his teachings were given. His teachings were given to the church, and it did not exist in the church. The Jews, to whom his teachings were confined, were not guilty of it, how could he condemn it in them?

vocates is a very strong argument that these men do not believe the apostles taught Slavery. Slave owners are willing you should preach what the Bible enjoins on the servant to their slaves, but he had better be out of Dixie if he ventures to preach what the scriptures enjoin on the master. What stronger argument can we have that the Bible does not justify Slavery?

That we may see how much the argument is worth, let us collate it with other passages. "But I say unto you, love your enemies, bless them that curse you, do good to them that hate you, and pray for them which despitefully use you, and persecute you." Math. v. 44. " Let every soul be subject unto the higher powers." Rom. xiii. 1.

Do these commands approve or justify enmity, hate, persecution, cursing, and despiteful abuse? Does obedience to a bad government justify bad government? The apostles commanded obedience to the Roman government, a government tolerating persecution for Christianity, feeding Christians to wild beasts, burning, torturing them, a government that gave the father power to kill his children, the husband his wife, and enjoined the death of hundreds or thousands of slaves for the murder of the master; does his command to be obedient and serve such a government, approve or sanction it? Just as much as his commands to be obedient to a master who violates the laws of God and nature, sanctions such a master, or such a system.

2d. That slavery is not a good condition to be in, and therefore it is not good to hold a man in it. "If thou mayest be made free, use it rather." 1. Cor. vii. 21. If you cannot be free it is not your fault, but the fault of another—if you can be, it is your duty to be free. If it is the slave's duty to be free, it is every man's duty not to enslave him Slavery is not as good a state as freedom; then every man is guilty of a wrong who forces such a state. The apostle plainly declares that Slavery is not as good a state for men as freedom, then how can he justify any for forcing this worse state on men? It is no where justified by Christ or his apostles.

3d. The effect of Bible teaching, of Christianity, is to destroy Slavery; how then could it be that Christ and his apostles taught it to be right? The converted heathen gave freedom to their slaves. Owners of slaves when converted, manumitted their slaves in hundreds, and it is said thousands, as inconsistent with the principles of their new religion. In the days of Constantine by an order of the Emperor it was done in the church and before the whole congregation. The real Bible portion of the world objected strongly against American Slavery, when introduced by enslaving the Indians. Las Casas "Rejected with indignation the idea, that any race of men was born to servitude, as irreligious, and inhuman." Rob. Am. 1, book III. It was the Bible in England which brought it to an end in the West Indies. It was Bible teaching in New England and Atlantic States, which banished it from every State where it existed, North of Mason and Dixon's line. The result of Bible teaching, if practiced, would be just what it was in the case of Onesimus, and what Paul exhorted Philemon to, the servant set free, and received as a brother beloved. Here is a sample of New Testament teaching, and practice. Paul tells Philemon he *might enjoin* him as a *Christian*, yet for love's sake, he beseeches him as a Christian brother, to receive his servant—but *not as a servant or slave*, but a brother, beloved. Taking Paul's Epistle to Philemon as their guide, how many Christians would hold slaves? Nay —how many *could?* Paul says he might *command* as an inspired apostle, what he asks Philemon to do—*not* to hold Onesimus as a slave, but regard him above a slave—a brother—an equal by the law of Christianity. If this is the law of Christianity, who then pleads Christianity to justify American Slavery? Phil. verses 8, 10—16. A Missionary in the West Indies before the abolition of Slavery there, was charged with reading an inflammatory chapter from the Bible to his congregation. It might have been true, for the Bible has many such chapters, and as offensive to our slaveholders as to the West Indians.

Great numbers in every age, since Christ's advent can

say, with Cochin, "*I owe to Christianity the horror with which Slavery inspires me.*"

4th. The apostles place our Slavery among the worst crimes. 1. Tim. i. 9—10, in enumerating things against which the law is ordained he specifies, the " profane, murderers of fathers and mothers, man-slayers, whoremongers, *men-stealers*, liars, and perjured persons." Our Slavery is founded in man-stealing, and it will be found to embrace all this catalogue of crime, profanity, murdering fathers and mothers, man-slaying, whoredom, lying and perjury. John Wesley expressed very briefly what Paul particularizes, "Slavery is the sum of all villanies." There is not a crime forbidden in the Bible, which American Slavery does not tolerate and practice.

There are hard problems in ethics and some men's system of theology, the solving of which would confer a favor on the unskilled and dull of apprehension. I have not been able to solve these, and will acknowledge my obligations to any one who will.

1st. How it is that the Bible teaches Slavery, and yet slave owners will not allow it to be taught to their slaves. Slaveholders, and the advocates of Slavery are very sure the Bible teaches Slavery, and yet Slavery makes it a crime to teach a slave to read the Bible. Are they afraid their slaves will find out it is a sin to be free? Or that God made them for slaves, and doomed them to this state?

2d. How it is that Slavery is good, and yet productive of untold evils; good, and yet always ends in mischief. In nearly every State or kingdom where it has not been abolished by law, it has ended in civil wars, insurrections, mobs, &c., as in Greece, Rome, Hayti, and the United States. What a Southern father told his children would be the result of Slavery in this country, "That the sun of Slavery would set in blood," was predicted from the history of Slavery and oppression in other countries. This has been its history. We need not go abroad to know what demoralization, violation of the decencies and amenities of life, brutalities and cruelties it breeds. We have all these and every sin forbidden in the decalogue, as the result of it in our land. God approves slavery, His word teaches it, and His providence is always against it, from the day He drowned the Egyptians in the Red Sea till to-day, when He is drowning American Slavery "in destruction and perdition." How is this accounted for?

3d. How is it, that God has implanted in the human soul a desire for freedom, a fact which every one knows in his own experience, and yet created men to be slaves? Does God make such contradictions, or is the desire of freedom a part of Adam's sin?

4th. How is it that the Bible teaches Slavery, and yet wherever the Bible goes, Slavery is abolished. It universally prevailed in the heathen world at the coming of Christ, but did not prevail among the Jews, and it disappeared from the heathen world wherever the Bible was introduced, and believed as the word of God.

5th. Slavery is a Divine institution—a Bible institution ordained and taught by prophets and apostles, then how is it, that nearly all good men in every age, have been opposed to it? and such a majority of bad men are in favor of it? To-day, ninety-nine out of one hundred of all Evangelical Ministers throughout Christendom, are opposed to it, at least those who have not an interest in it, or are not in some way involved in it. The *scandal* of being *abolitionists* has belonged to Christians in all ages, and the glory of approving and justifying Slavery, to but very few. Thousands in this country are heartily opposed to the system, who have hitherto been opposed to meddling with it in the States, until those States have sought to enforce it on the country, and to found a slave empire, have waged war on the Government. This has been my position until this war. Though called an abolitionist, I have not till lately been entitled to the credit, or scandal, as you please to regard it. I am now thoroughly converted, and have no scruples in placing it where Paul has, among the worst of crimes, and am so far a Wesleyan as to believe with the author of Wesleyanism, that "it is the sum of all villainies." "A Divine Institution!" a divine institution for man-stealing—for robbing a man of his rights, for adultery per force, and by the right of the master—for traffic in the souls and bodies of men! All this, and a thousand other things of like character, and some worse, by the grace of God, to be sure! By the grace of God to whom? Why, to the slave himself we are told! To the man who is knocked down, manacled, and sold to men who work them as they do oxen, deny them the Bible, keep them in ignorance, whip and torture them to their heart's content! To woman, whom the good and gracious system, subjects to the lusts of the master, and to see their own offspring sold at the master's pleasure for a cotton plantation! What a God the God of Slavery must be! and the men who conceived such a being! The day is coming when the world will be at a loss to understand what could have been the condition of society when such sentiments were tolerated or believed.

In conclusion, I have no apology to offer for this sermon, the text was laid upon the desk, and I was requested to preach from it; and, I judged, not by an abolitionist or an anti-slavery man, for they are not apt to fasten their attention on such texts, or feel any special favor for them. I have not preached it therefore, to gratify anti-slavery men, nor with any design or desire to wound the feelings of those who differ with me. This I would gladly avoid. It is always more or less painful to preach what I know friends dislike to hear. I love my friends, and pray God to give me grace to love my enemies. For several years past, the question of duty and friendship have had a constant struggle in my mind. I have hesitated, pondered and prayed, to know what I should do. Friends on the one hand, and the question of duty on the other—friends who had been such for twenty long years, and the claims as I believed of my country, of patriotism, of religion, of my vows as a minister, to be faithful to the truth and my fears of the judgment on the other, have given me some wakeful hours, and no small agitation and anxiety. I would not be understood that this was entirely on my own account—the welfare, the unity, and prosperity of the church over which God has placed me, had something to do in the matter. The church is worth many such things as myself. Every member is as precious in the eye of God as myself, and I would not offend one of Christ's little ones. I fear the millstone. I have read the maledictions of politicians on the floor of Congress against ministers, and heard them in the streets by the drunken tools of politicians, for meddling with politics, when praying for our country, for the Government, was the sin, when the mere mention of Slavery was politics, and this by men who branded every man as an abolitionist who was not heart and hand for Slavery. These were not my trouble, but friends in the fold of Christ—who, perhaps, were his in the covenant of redemption, but were misled, were in the dark on the subject, and who suffered the blindness, perhaps in the providence of God to rebuke my own unfaithfulness, and be a thorn in the flesh to keep me sensitive to duty, and cure pride. The effect has been a careful examination as to duty on the subject now discussed, and to the church and government. I have not been able to prove to my satisfaction, that a Christian Minister may not be, or *ought* not to be a patriot, love his country, pray for the Government; or that his patriotism should be less at a time above all others when patriotism is demanded, or his prayers or efforts be less when his country is in danger, and great efforts made to overthrow the Government. I am convinced that a *Christian must be a patriot,* and none the less for being a *minister;* that in time of need, as I conceive the present to be, he ought to be willing to make any sacrifice of time, labor, friends, money, and life, if need be. A good Government is God's gift, and the best gift to men for this world, and ours is unquestionably the best the world has, or perhaps ever has had, being founded on the principle of universal freedom to all, and in which all help to govern; the very kind of government indeed, which God himself gave to his own chosen people; separate tribes, but one general government; the tribes distinct, and yet one; a written Constitution for each State, and a National one; laws enacted by the people, rulers and judges chosen by the people, and from among the people, and full provision made for amending and correcting any bad law, and the removal of every bad magistrate, and redressing every wrong What more can any people ask? What better can God do for them in the bestowment of a government? Being fully pursuaded of these facts, I have preached some four patriotic sermons since the war began, in my feeble way trying to convince my people of these truths, and our duties in connection with them. Holding these sentiments, I cannot but regard every man in error who lightly esteems the rich boon which God has conferred on us in the Government he has given us ; and every man who, from party motives, or any other, takes part against the Government or those laboring to sustain it against this rebellion, as the enemies of the country, my enemies and yours ; and every system, and everything which endangers the peace and perpetuity of this Government as mischievous, wrong, wicked. Such I regard Slavery. It is at the bottom of, and the author— the sole cause of this war. As a patriot then, I ought to hate Slavery ; it has sought, and is now struggling to destroy my country ; as a friend to good Government, I ought to hate it ; it has undermined and fired the train, to blow to fragments, the best Government in the world. As the friend of universal, civil, and religious liberty, I ought to hate it ; it is the monster tyrant that seeks the destruction of human liberty, and to extend its empire of darkness and oppression over the world. As the friend of education, of light and intelligence, I ought to hate it ; it has opposed and obstructed all these as far as it could. As a Christian, I ought to hate it, and all kinds of oppression; all the prophets, and good men of every age, have been its enemies. As a minister of the gospel of peace, I ought to be its enemy ; it has commenced, and is now waging a bloody, cruel, causeless and barbarous war, of which savages ought to be ashamed. As a philanthropist, I ought to abominate it ; what wrong has it not inflicted on men? What thousands, yea what millions, has it robbed and murdered, and cast to the sharks of the ocean? No, there is not a Christian emotion in the soul of man, not a kind or a right emotion, which is not opposed to American Slavery. We rejoice in the belief that its day of doom has come, that the hand is seen writing on the wall, that the river is turned, and the army of deliverance is entering "the two-leaved gates," and soon God's captives shall be set free, and the American Belshazzar and his impious Lords be slain, and Babylon be utterly destroyed. A "voice from heaven," the providence of God, the signs of the times, say to God's people, "Come out of her, my people, that ye be not partakers of her sins, and that ye receive not of her plagues. For her sins have reached unto heaven, and God hath remembered her iniquities. Reward her according to her works ; in the cup which she hath filled, fill to her double. How much she hath glorified herself and lived deliciously, so much torment and sorrow give her ; for she saith in her heart, I sit a queen, and am no widow, and shall see no sorrow. Therefore shall her plagues come in one day, death, and mourning, and famine ; and she shall be utterly burned with fire, for strong is the Lord God who judgeth her."